The Country Tea Rose Quilt

Design by Cheryl A. Benner
Text by Rachel T. Pellman

Good Books

Intercourse, PA 17534

Acknowledgments

Design by Cheryl A. Benner

Cover and color photography by Jonathan Charles

The Country Tea Rose Quilt

© 1993 by Good Books, Intercourse, PA 17534

International Standard Book Number: 1-56148-097-5

Library of Congress Catalog Card Number:

93-33953

Library of Congress Cataloging-in-Publication Data

Benner, Cheryl A, 1962

The country tea rose quilt / design by Cheryl A. Benner ; text by Rachel
T. Pellman.

    p . cm.

  ISBN 1-56148-097-5 : $12.95

  1. Quilting--Patterns. 2. Applique--Patterns. 3. Roses in art.
I. Pellman, Rachel T. (Rachel Thomas) II. Title.

TT835.B354 1993

746.9′7041-dc20   93-33953

                                         CIP

Table of Contents

The Country Tea Rose Quilt

Bold yet delicate, traditional yet new, The Country Tea Rose quilt is yet another in the line of quilt patterns from The Old Country Store.

The inspiration for the pieced design comes from the traditional Center Diamond pattern. A delicate bouquet of tea roses floats exquisitely in this deeply colored field. Surrounding the diamond are two inner borders. The first is covered with a leafy applique vine and the second extends beyond the edges of the bed to join a pieced border framing the whole. The pieced angular border provides a complementary balance for the flowing lines of the applique motifs.

A wide exterior border is highlighted on each lower corner with a spray of tea rose flowers.

Simple crosshatch quilting covers the entire background sections, and each applique flower is enhanced with outline quilting.

The quilt is finished with a gently zigzagged bound edge.

Though the overall finished look is somewhat complex, the Country Tea Rose pattern does not require extensive experience in quiltmaking.

For those who wish to use the design for a smaller project, the center section can be appliqued and framed with a border to make a wallhanging-size quilt.

The Tea Rose quilts pictured in this book are done in deep, rich colors and incorporate large floral fabrics, currently popular with quiltmakers. But part of the wonder of quiltmaking is that quilters interpret and execute patterns following their own preferences. The quilt you make from this pattern will be distinctly yours. We wish we could see each of them. Enjoy both the process and your finished product!

How to Begin

Read the following instructions thoroughly before beginning work on your quilt.

Wash all fabrics before cutting them. This process will both preshrink and test them for colorfastness. If the fabric is not colorfast after one washing, repeat the washings until the water remains clear, or replace the cloth with another fabric. If fabrics are wrinkled after washing and drying, iron them before using them.

Fabrics suitable for quilting are generally lightweight, tightly woven cotton and cotton/polyester blends. They should not unravel easily and should not hold excessive wrinkles when squeezed and released. Because of the hours of time required to make a quilt, it is worth investing in high quality fabrics.

Fabric requirements given here are for standard 45" wide fabric. If you use wider or more narrow fabrics, calculate the variations you will need.

All seams are sewn using ¼" seam allowances. Measurements given include seam allowances except for applique pieces (see "Making Templates" on page 9).

Applique Quilts

Preparing Background Fabric for Appliqueing

When you purchase fabric for the background and borders, buy the total amount you need from one bolt of fabric. This will ensure that all the patches and borders will be the same shade. Dye lots can vary significantly from bolt to bolt of fabric, and those differences are emphasized when placed next to each other in a quilt top.

Cutting diagrams are shown to make the most efficient use of fabric. Label each piece after it is cut. Mark right and wrong sides of fabric as well.

So that you know where to place the applique pieces on the background piece, trace the applique design lightly on the right side of the background fabric before beginning to stitch. Even though the applique pieces will be laid over these markings and stitched in place, it is important to mark these lines as lightly as possible. Center the applique designs on the background sections.

The placement of the applique on the pillow throw is an exception to that rule. Center that applique from side to side, but place it nearer the top of the quilt so that there is extra fullness for tucking the quilt under the pillows. The space from the top of the pillow throw section to the highest point of the applique design should measure about 10 inches.

When doing applique on background pieces with bias edges (such as triangular corners) it is best to mark the triangular shapes onto the background fabric and do the applique **before** cutting along the bias edges. The handling of the fabric during the appliquing process can easily stretch and distort the bias edges, making them difficult to piece accurately if they were cut prior to the appliquing.

Making Templates

Make templates from pattern pieces printed in this book, using material that will not wear along the edges from repeated tracing. Cardboard is suitable for pieces being traced only a few times. Plastic lids or the sides of plastic cartons work well for templates that will be used repeatedly. Quilt supply shops and art supply stores carry sheets of plastic that work well for template-making.

Quiltmaking demands precision. Remember that as you begin marking! First, test the template you have made against the original printed pattern for accuracy. The applique templates are given in the actual size, without seam allowances. Trace them that way. Then trace them on the right side of the fabric, but spaced far enough apart so that you can cut them approximately ¼" outside the marked lines. The traced line is the fold line, indicating the exact shape of the applique piece. Since these lines are on the right side of the fabric and will be on the folded edge, make the markings as light as possible.

Each applique piece needs to be traced separately (rather than having the fabric doubled), so the fold line is marked on each one. Note, too, that since some of the pieces face in opposite directions, some will need to be traced pointing in one direction and some will need to be traced pointing the opposite way (see illustration).

Appliqueing

Begin by appliqueing the cut-out fabric pieces, one at a time, over the placement lines drawn onto the background fabric pieces. Be alert to the sequence in which the pieces are applied, so that sections which overlap each other are done in proper order. For example, when you do the center patch of the Country Tea Rose quilt, you will need to do lower portions of the roses first. Upper petals overlay lower ones. In cases where a portion of an applique piece is covered by another, the section being covered does not need to be stitched, since it will be held in place by the stitches of the section that lies over it.

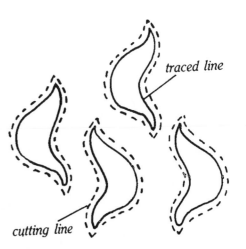

traced line

cutting line

Applique templates should be traced on the right side of the fabric, but spaced far enough apart so they can be cut approximately ¼" outside the marked line. Some pieces face in opposite directions and need to be traced that way.

9

The applique stitch is a tiny, tight stitch that goes through the background fabric and emerges to catch only a few threads of the appliqued piece along the fold line.

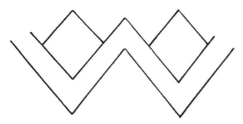

Quilting lines are marked on the surface of the quilt top. Markings should be as light as possible so they are easily seen for quilting, yet do not distract when the quilting is completed.

Appliqueing is not difficult, but it does require patience and precision. The best applique work has perfectly smooth curves and sharply defined points. To achieve this, stitches must be very small and tight. First, pin the piece being appliqued to the outline on the background piece. Using thread that matches the piece being applied, stitch the piece to the background section, folding the seam allowance under to the traced line on the applique piece. Fold under only a tiny section at a time.

The applique stitch is a running stitch, going through the background fabric and emerging to catch only a few threads of the appliqued piece along the folded line. Make your needle re-enter the background piece for the next stitch at almost the same place it emerged, creating a stitch so small that it is almost invisible along the edge of the appliqued piece. Stitches on the underside of the background fabric should be about ⅛" long.

To form sharp points, fold in one side and stitch almost to the end of the point. Fold in the opposite side to form the point and push the excess seam allowance under the point of the needle. You may trim the excess seam allowance to eliminate bulk. Stitch tightly.

To form smooth curves, clip along the curves to the fold line. Fold under while stitching, using the needle to push under the seam allowances.

Assembling the Appliqued Quilt Top

When all your applique work is completed, you are ready to assemble the patches. See the diagram on page 15. Applique work on the corners will need to be completed after the top is assembled.

Quilting on Applique and Pieced Quilts

Marking Quilting Designs

Quilting designs are marked on the surface of the quilt top. A lead pencil provides a thin line and, if used with very little pressure, creates markings that are easily seen for quilting, yet do not distract when the quilt is completed. There are numerous marking pencils on the market, as well as chalk markers. Test whatever you choose on a scrap piece of fabric to be sure it performs as promised. Remember, quilting lines are not obliterated by quilting stitches, so make the lines light or removable.

Quilting

A quilt consists of three layers—the back or underside of the quilt, the batting, and the top, which is the appliqued layer. Quilting stitches follow a decorative pattern, piercing through all three layers of the quilt "sandwich" and holding it together.

Many quilters prefer to stretch their quilts into large quilting frames. These are built so that the finished area of the quilt can be rolled up as work on it progresses. This type of frame allows space for several quilters to work on the same quilt and is used at quilting bees. Smaller hoops can be used to quilt small sections at a time. If you use one of the smaller frames, it is important that you first stretch the three layers of the quilt in the frame, then baste them securely together to prevent puckering.

The quilting stitch is a simple running stitch. Quilting needles are called "betweens" and are shorter than "sharps," which are regular handsewing needles. The higher the number, the smaller the needle. Many quilters prefer a size 8 or 9 needle.

Quilting is done with a single strand of quilting thread. Knot the thread and insert the needle through the top layer, about one inch away from the point where quilting should emerge on a marked quilting line. Gently tug the knot through the fabric so it is hidden between the layers. Then bring the needle up through the quilt top, going through all layers of the quilt.

Keep one hand under the quilt to feel when the needle has successfully penetrated all layers and to help guide the needle back up to the surface. Your upper hand receives the needle and repeats the process. It is possible to stack as many as five stitches on the needle before pulling the thread through. However, when you work curves, you have smoother results if you stack fewer stitches. Pull the quilting stitches taut but not so tight as to pucker the fabric. When you have used the entire length of thread, reinforce the stitching with a tiny backstitch. Then reinsert the needle in the top layer, push it through for a long stitch, pull it out and clip the thread.

The goal in quilting is to have straight, even stitches that are of equal length on both the top and bottom of the quilt. That achievement comes with hours of practice!

When you quilt the applique patches, simply outline the applique designs. This outline quilting will accent the applique section and cause it to appear slightly puffed.

A quilt is a sandwich of three layers—the quilt back, the batting, and the quilt top—all held together by the quilting stitches.

Mitering Corners

Step 1

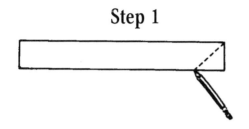

Measure in from each end the exact number of inches as the border width. Draw a diagonal line from that point to the outer corner. Cut along angled line.

Step 2

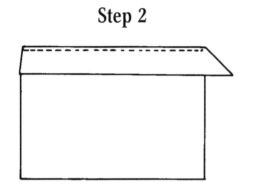

Stitch borders to quilt, leaving a ¼" seam allowance open at each mitered end.

Step 3

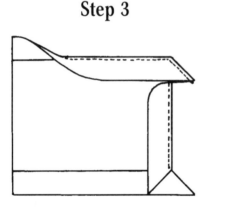

Stitch across the open ends of the corners from the inside corner to the outer edge.

Binding

The final stage in completing a quilt is the binding, which finishes the quilt's raw edge. When binding a non-straight-edged quilt, cut the binding strips on the bias. This allows more flex and stretch around curves. To cut on the bias, cut the fabric at a 45 degree angle to the straight of grain.

A double thickness of binding on the edge of the quilt gives it additional strength and durability. To create a double binding, cut the binding strips 2-2½" wide. Sew strips together to form a continuous length of binding.

When binding a quilt with zigzag edges, it is easier to attach the binding before cutting the zigzag edge. To do so, baste the raw edges of the quilt together. Mark but do not cut the jagged border. Using a ¼" seam allowance, sew the binding along the marked edge, pivoting at the end of each point to create a sharp turn. Trim the zigzags even with the edge of the binding. Wrap the binding around to the back, enclosing the raw edges and covering the stitch line. Slipstitch in place with thread that matches the color of the binding fabric.

To Display Quilts

Wall quilts can be hung in various ways. You can simply tack the quilt directly to the wall. However, this is potentially damaging to both quilt and wall. Except for a permanent hanging, this is probably not the best way.

Another option is to hang the quilt like a painting. To do this, make a narrow sleeve from matching fabric and handsew it to the upper edge of the quilt along the back. Insert a dowel rod through the sleeve and hang the rod by wire or nylon string.

The quilt can also be hung on a frame. This method requires velcro or fabric to be attached to the frame itself. If you choose velcro, staple one side to the frame. Handsew the opposite velcro on the edges of the quilt, then attach the quilt carefully to the velcro on the frame. If you attach fabric to the frame, handstitch the quilt to the frame itself.

Quilts can also be mounted inside plexiglas by a professional framery. This method, often reserved for antique quilts, can provide an acid-free, dirt-free and, with special plexiglas, a sun-proof environment for your quilt.

Other Projects

The Country Tea Rose pattern is adaptable to other projects as well. To make a wallhanging, follow the instructions for appliqueing but use only the center patch. Add a border with decorative quilting for a lovely wallhanging.

Borders on wallhangings may be mitered for a more tailored look. See the illustration on page 12 for instructions on mitered corners.

Pillows can also be made by using the applique motif from the border corner of the quilt. Applique the motif on to a background square, and then quilt the patch. To make the back of the pillow, cut a square equal in size to the front in either matching or contrasting fabric.

Make a ruffle using one of the fabrics used in the applique design. To make the ruffle, cut three strips of fabric measuring 4 ½" x 45" each. Sew these strips together to form a continuous length. Bring the two ends together, wrong sides together, and stitch to create a fabric circle. Fold the fabric circle in half with wrong sides together. Stitch along the raw edge of the entire circumference of the circle using a long running stitch. Gather the circle to fit around the edges of the quilted top. Pin the ruffle to the pillow top with raw edges even, and spread the gathers evenly throughout. Baste the ruffle to the pillow top. With right sides together and the ruffle sandwiched between the layers, pin the back to the pillow top. Stitch back to top through all layers, leaving a five-inch opening along one side. Trim the seams. Turn pillow right side out. Stuff pillow with polyester fiberfill. Slipstitch the opening.

Signing and Dating Quilts

To preserve history for future generations, sign and date the quilts you make. Include your initials and the year the quilt was made. This data can be added discreetly in a corner of the quilt. Embroider or quilt it among the quilting designs. Another alternative is to stitch or write the information on a separate piece of fabric and handstitch it to the back of the quilt. Whatever method you choose, this is an important and lasting part of finishing a quilt.

The Country Tea Rose Quilt
Cutting Layout for Queen-size or Double-size Quilt

Final size—approximately 92" x 112" • Measurements include seam allowances.

Total yardage for quilt back—8¾ yards

(Piece three 2¾-yard lengths of 45" fabric horizontally. This will make a back size of 99" x 135." Trim excess)

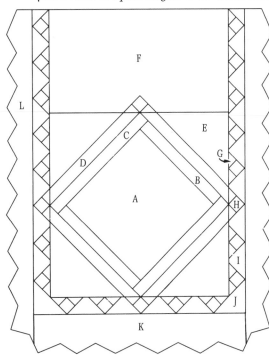

A—Center Diamond—cut one—34½" square

B—Inner Borders—cut two—4¾" x 35"

C—Inner Borders—cut two—4¾" x 43"

D—Outer Borders—cut four—4¾" x 43"

E—Corner Triangles—cut two squares and cut on the diagonal to form four triangles

F—Pillow Throw—cut one—36¼" x 60½"

G—Pieced Border Triangles—cut twenty-two squares and cut on the diagonal to form forty-four triangles

H—Pieced Border Squares—cut twenty-two— 4¾" square

I—Pieced Border Triangles—cut ten squares and cut on the diagonal to form twenty triangles

J—Corner Pieced Border Triangles—cut one square and cut on the diagonal to form two triangles

K—Bottom Border—cut one—10½" x 72½"

L—Side Borders—cut two—10½" x 112½"

Fabric Layout for Sections B, C, F, I, J, K, L (5 yards = 180")

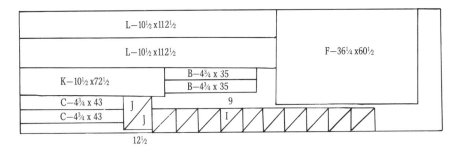

Yardage for Piecing
The Country Tea Rose Quilt

A, E—Center Diamond, Corner Triangles—2½ yards

B, C, F, I, J, K, L—Inner Borders, Pillow Throw, Corner Triangles, Side Borders, Bottom Border— 5 yards

D—Second Inner Border—¾ yard

G—Pieced Border Triangles—½ yard

Note: If Inner Border and Squares are alike, there will be no additional fabric needed, as squares can be cut from fabric left over from the border.

Yardage for Appliquing
The Country Tea Rose Quilt

Tea Rose Flowers—¼ yard each of six co-ordinated fabrics

Pointed Double Leaves—1/16 yard each of two fabrics

Leaves—½ yard each of solid and printed fabrics

Bias Tape for Stems—10½ yards

Assembly Instructions for the Country Tea Rose Quilt
Queen-size/Double-size

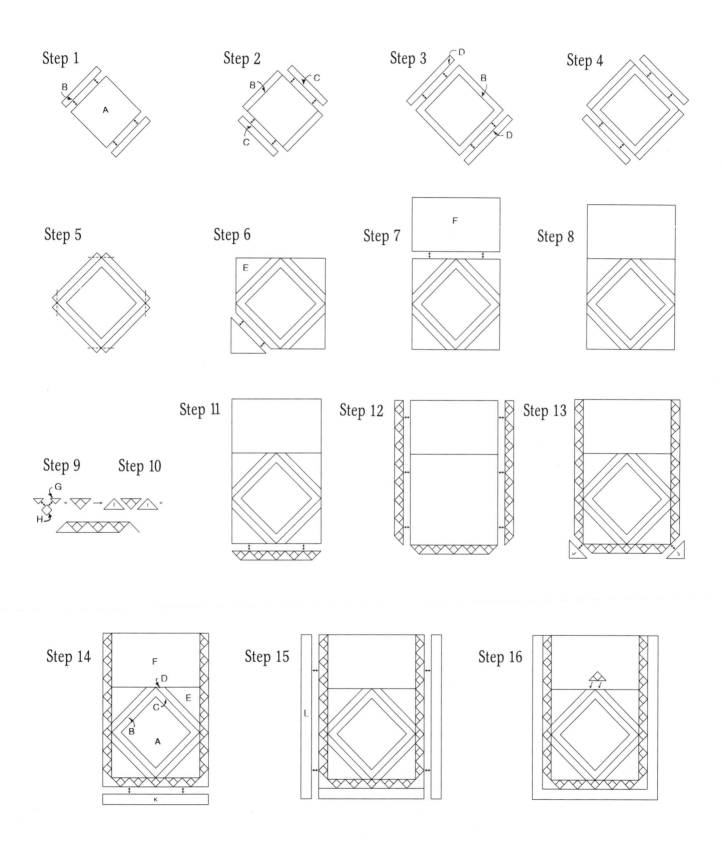

The Country Tea Rose Quilt Applique Templates
Center Diamond Patch

Note: Two separate fabrics make up each Heart Leaf.

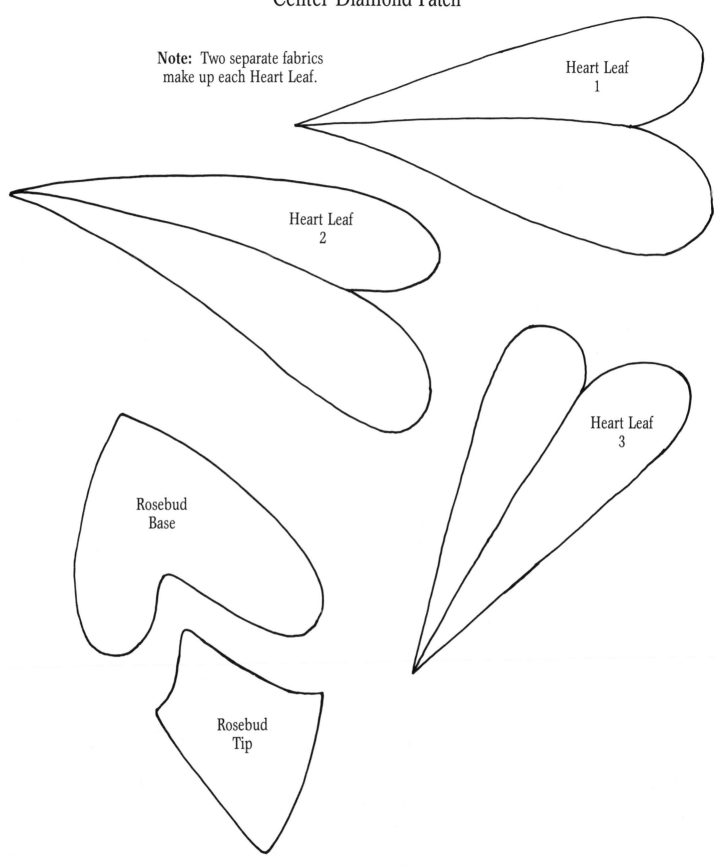

Heart Leaf 1

Heart Leaf 2

Heart Leaf 3

Rosebud Base

Rosebud Tip

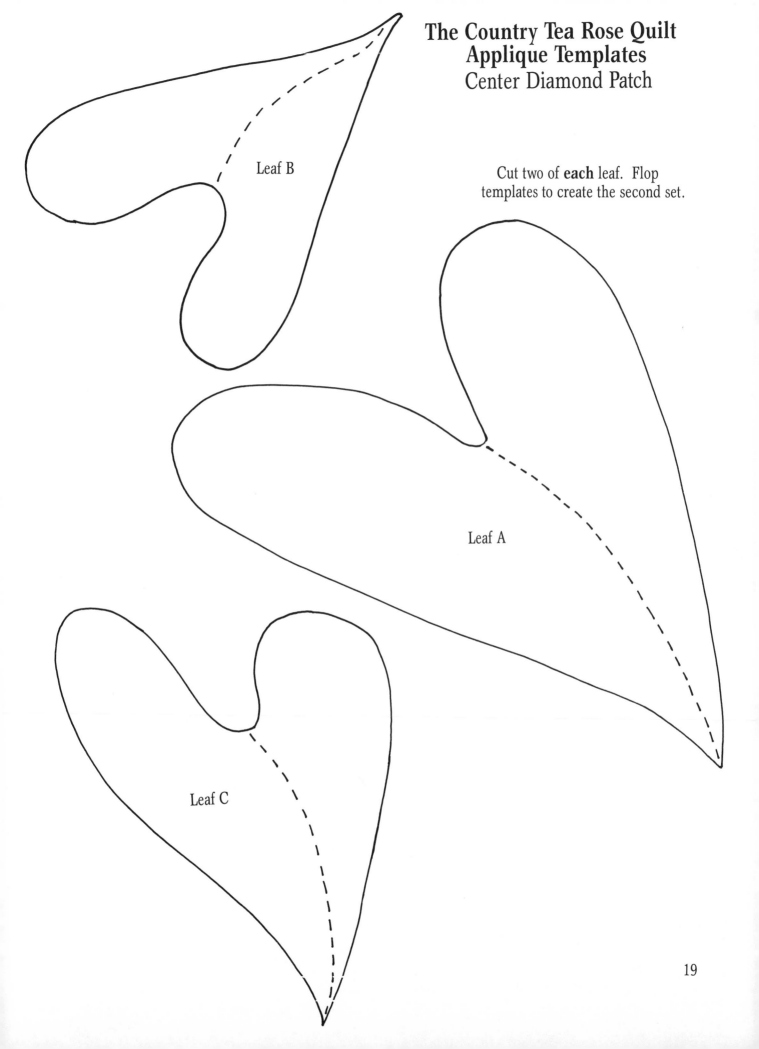

The Country Tea Rose Quilt
Applique Templates
Center Diamond Patch

Leaf B

Cut two of **each** leaf. Flop
templates to create the second set.

Leaf A

Leaf C

19

The Country Tea Rose Quilt Applique Templates
Center Diamond Patch

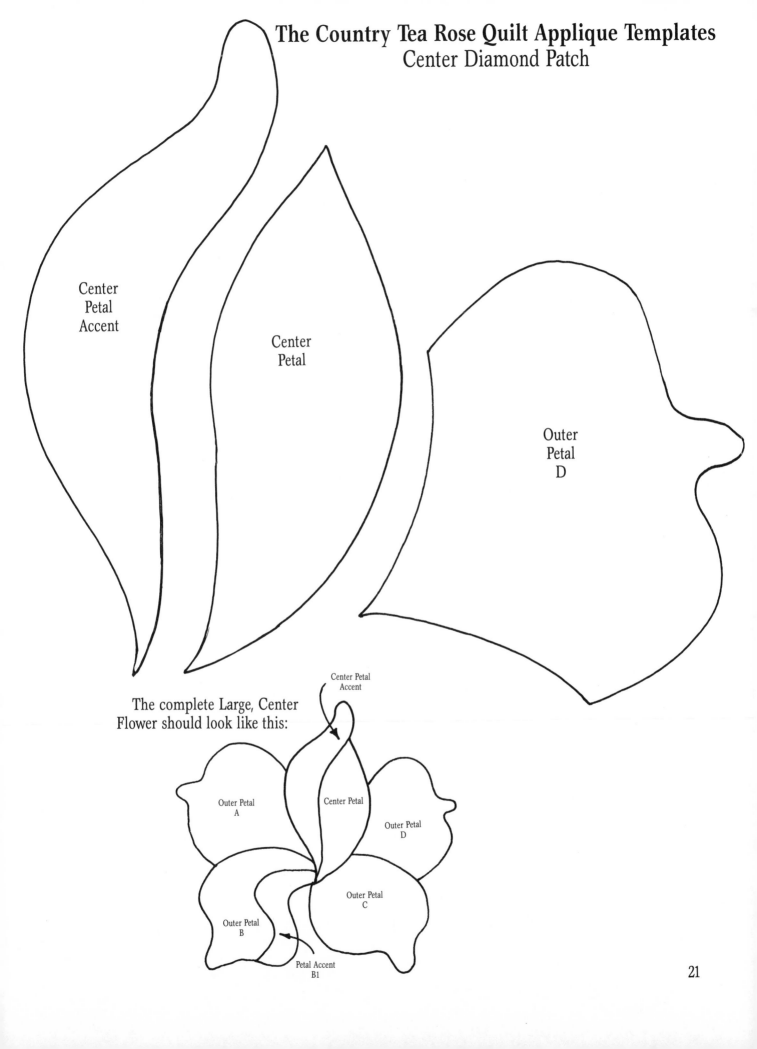

Center Petal Accent

Center Petal

Outer Petal D

The complete Large, Center Flower should look like this:

Center Petal Accent

Outer Petal A

Center Petal

Outer Petal D

Outer Petal C

Outer Petal B

Petal Accent B1

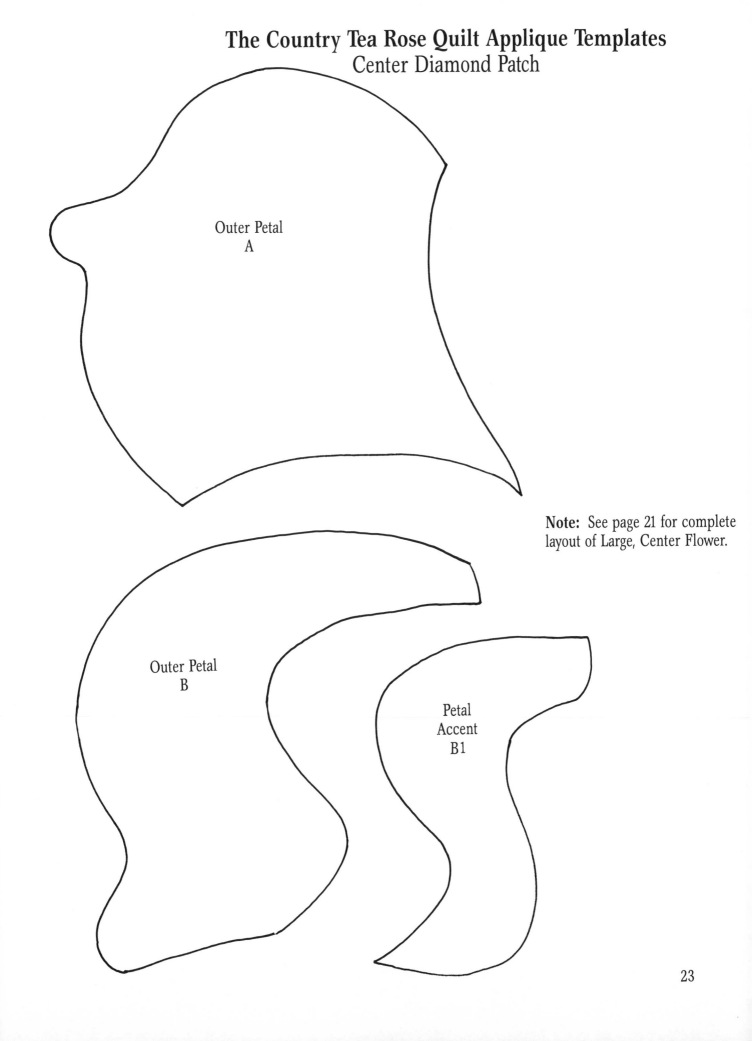

The Country Tea Rose Quilt Applique Templates
Center Diamond Patch

Outer Petal
A

Note: See page 21 for complete layout of Large, Center Flower.

Outer Petal
B

Petal
Accent
B1

The Country Tea Rose Quilt Applique Templates
Center Diamond Patch

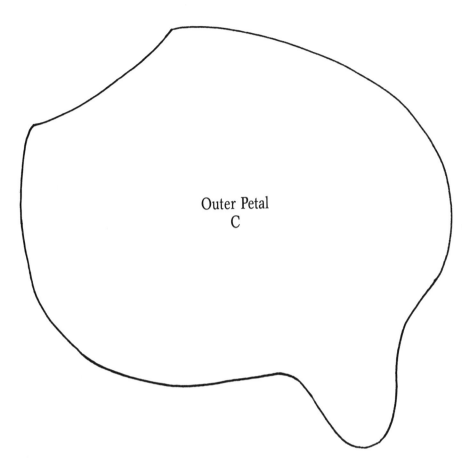

Outer Petal
C

Note: See page 21 for complete layout of Large, Center Flower.

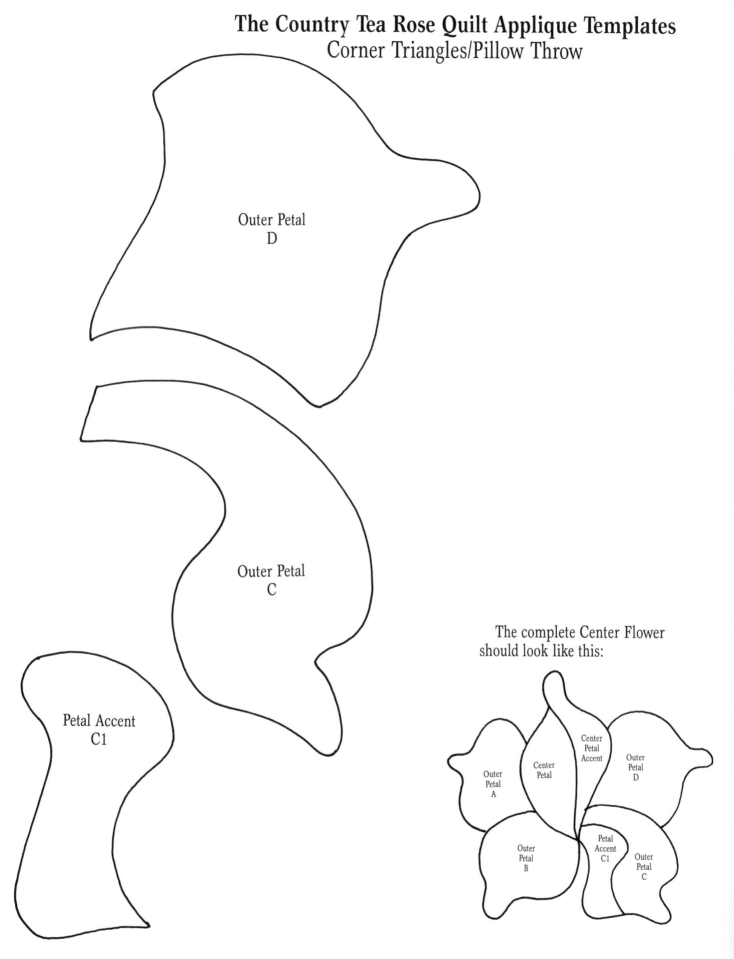

Outer Petal
D

Outer Petal
C

Petal Accent
C1

The complete Center Flower
should look like this:

Center
Petal
Accent

Center
Petal

Outer
Petal
A

Outer
Petal
D

Outer
Petal
B

Petal
Accent
C1

Outer
Petal
C

The Country Tea Rose Quilt Applique Templates
Corner Triangles/Pillow Throw

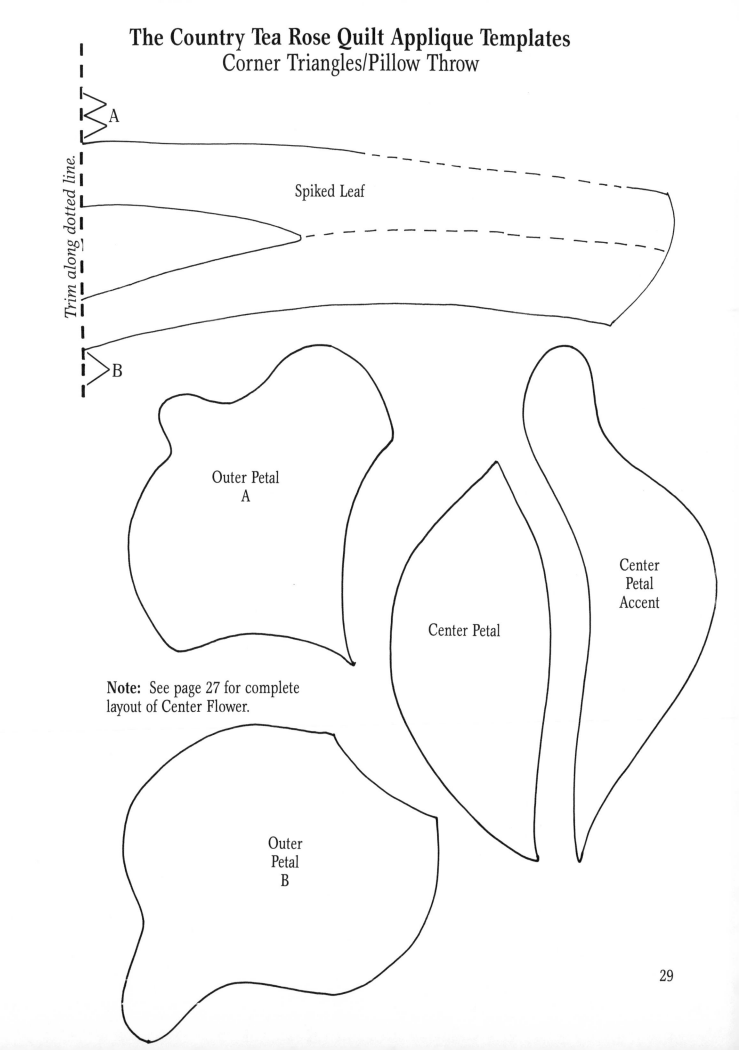

Trim along dotted line.

A

Spiked Leaf

B

Outer Petal
A

Center Petal

Center
Petal
Accent

Note: See page 27 for complete
layout of Center Flower.

Outer
Petal
B

29

The Country Tea Rose Quilt Applique Templates

Corner Triangles/Pillow Throw

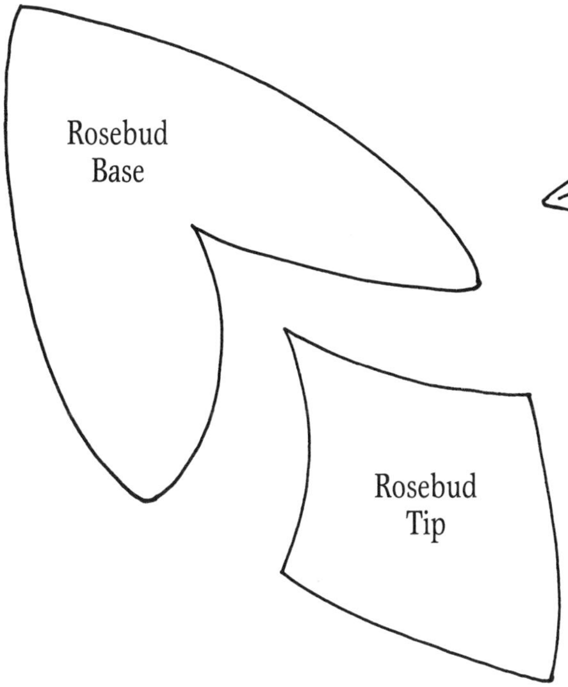
Rosebud Base
Rosebud Tip

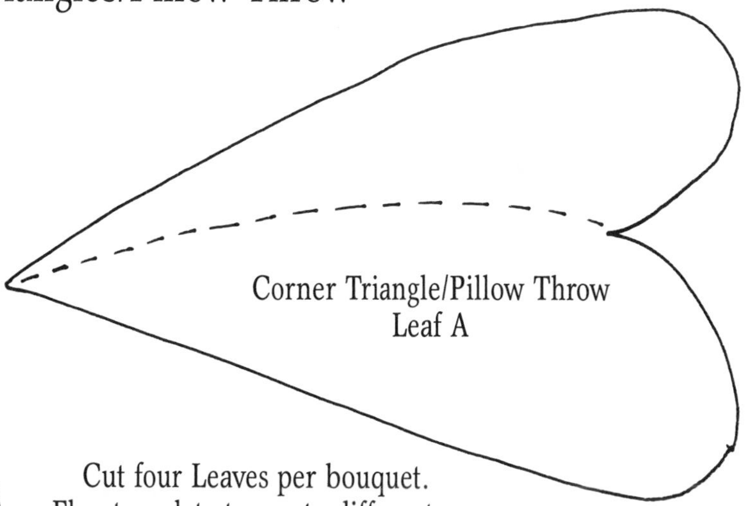
Corner Triangle/Pillow Throw
Leaf A

Cut four Leaves per bouquet.
Flop template to create different direction of Leaves.

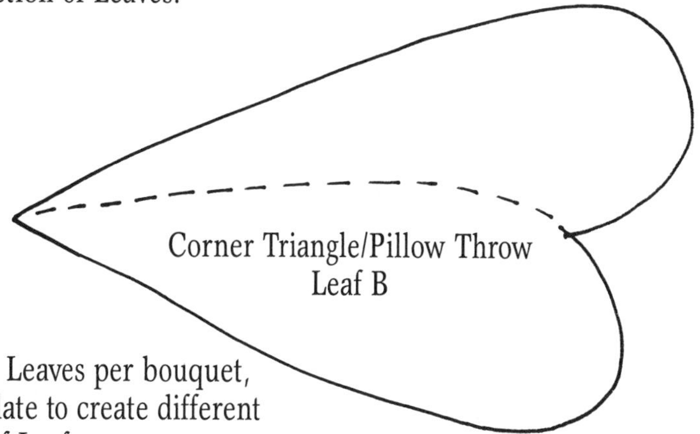
Corner Triangle/Pillow Throw
Leaf B

Cut two Leaves per bouquet,
Flop template to create different direction of Leaf.

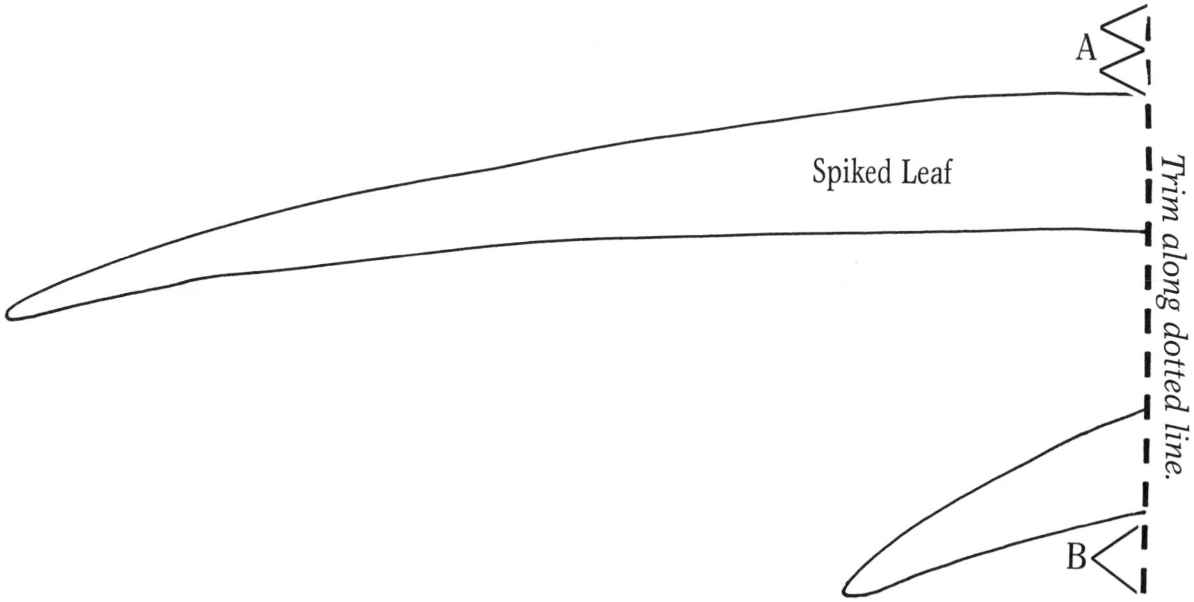
A
Spiked Leaf
Trim along dotted line.
B

The Country Tea Rose Quilt Applique Templates
Corner Border/Side Border

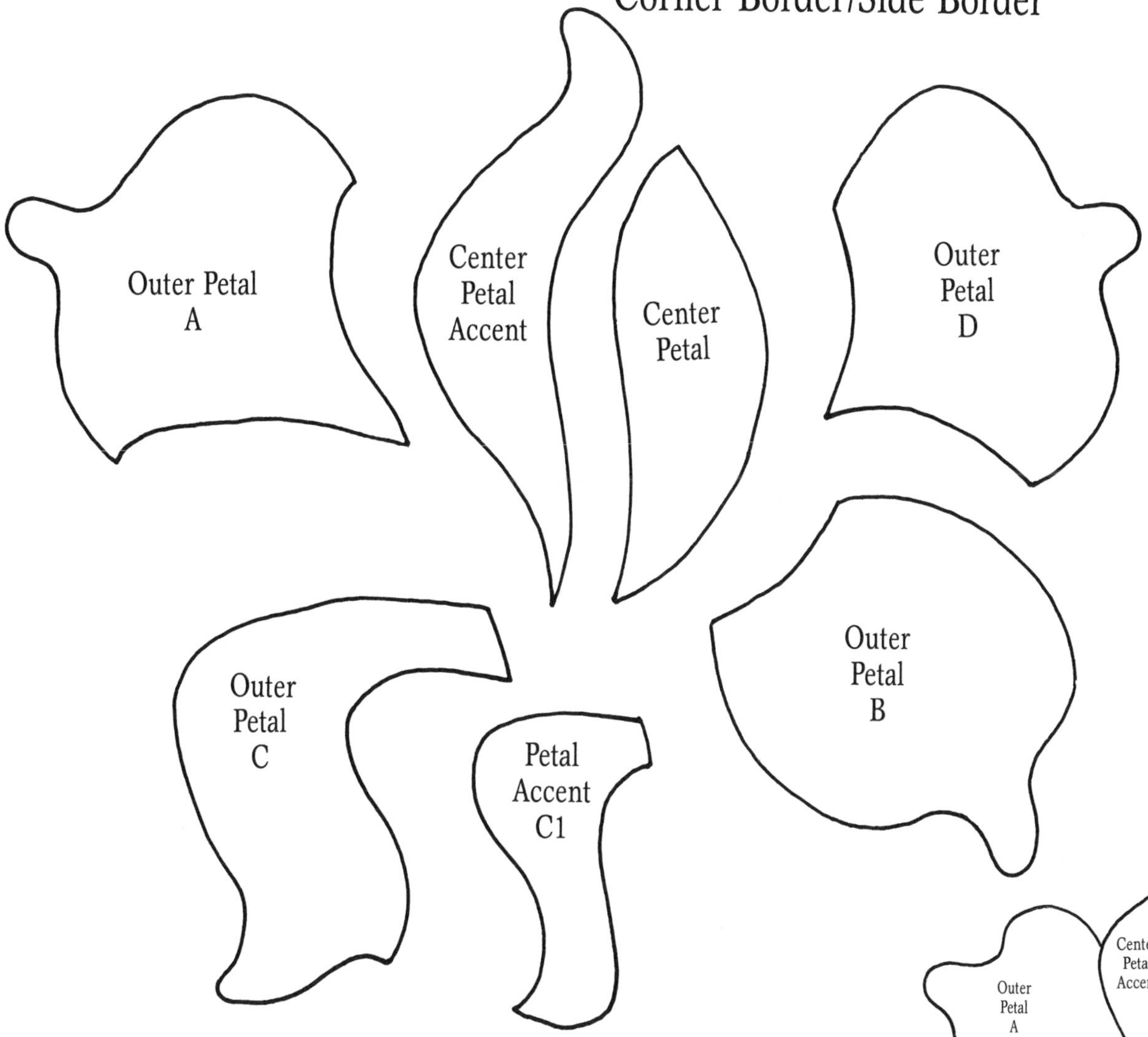

Outer Petal
A

Center
Petal
Accent

Center
Petal

Outer
Petal
D

Outer
Petal
C

Petal
Accent
C1

Outer
Petal
B

Cut two Leaves per bouquet,
Flop template to create different
direction of Leaf.

The complete Center Flower
should look like this:

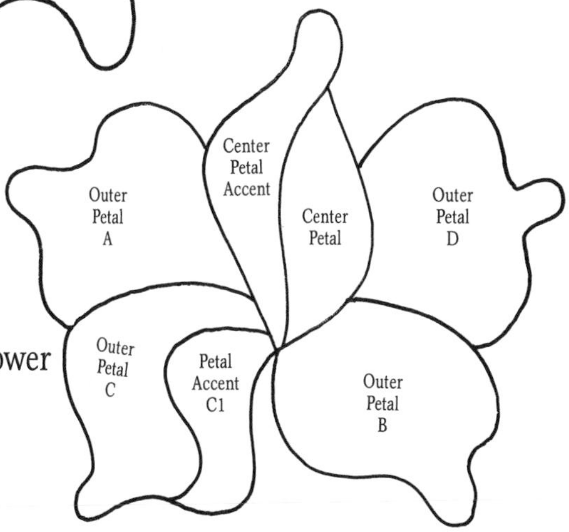

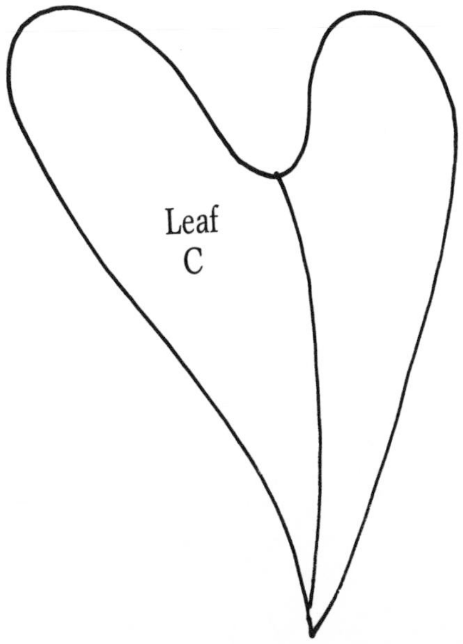

Outer
Petal
A

Center
Petal
Accent

Center
Petal

Outer
Petal
D

Outer
Petal
C

Petal
Accent
C1

Outer
Petal
B

Leaf
C

Cut four Leaves per bouquet.
Flop template to create different
direction of Leaves.

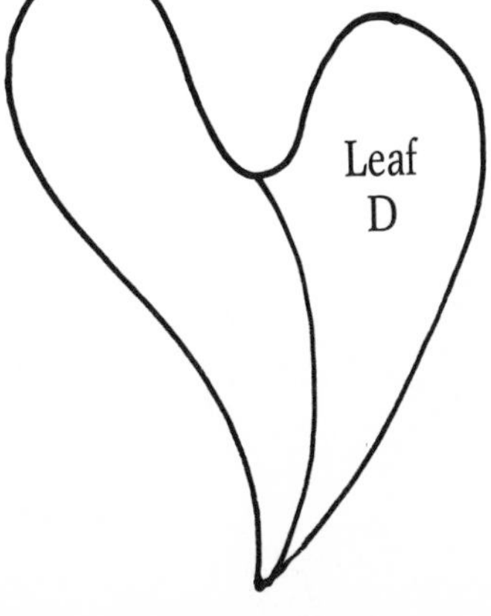

Leaf
D

33

The Country Tea Rose Quilt Applique Templates
Corner Border/Side Border

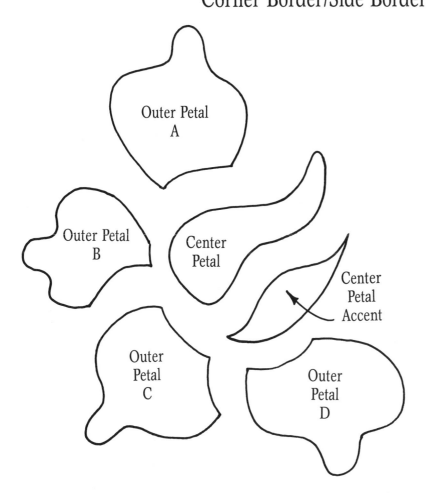

Outer Petal
A

Outer Petal
B

Center
Petal

Center
Petal
Accent

Outer
Petal
C

Outer
Petal
D

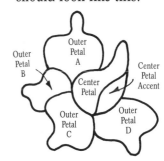

The complete Flower
should look like this:

Outer
Petal
B

Outer
Petal
A

Center
Petal

Center
Petal
Accent

Outer
Petal
C

Outer
Petal
D

Cut two Flowers per bouquet.
Flop template to create other
direction of Flower.

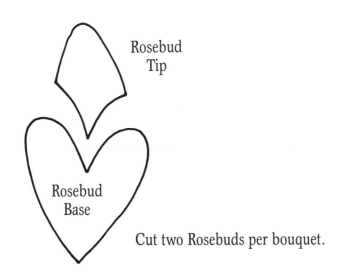

Rosebud
Tip

Rosebud
Base

Cut two Rosebuds per bouquet.

The Country Tea Rose Quilt Applique Layout
Ivy Vine Border

Trim along dotted line.

Use one Leaf as a template.
Continue vine to complete border.
Cut 7 Leaves for **each** panel.

37

Trim along dotted line.

To create the Center Diamond layout, connect corresponding letters and notches along dotted lines and tape. Completed layout will look like this:

CC

Trim along dotted line.

39

DD

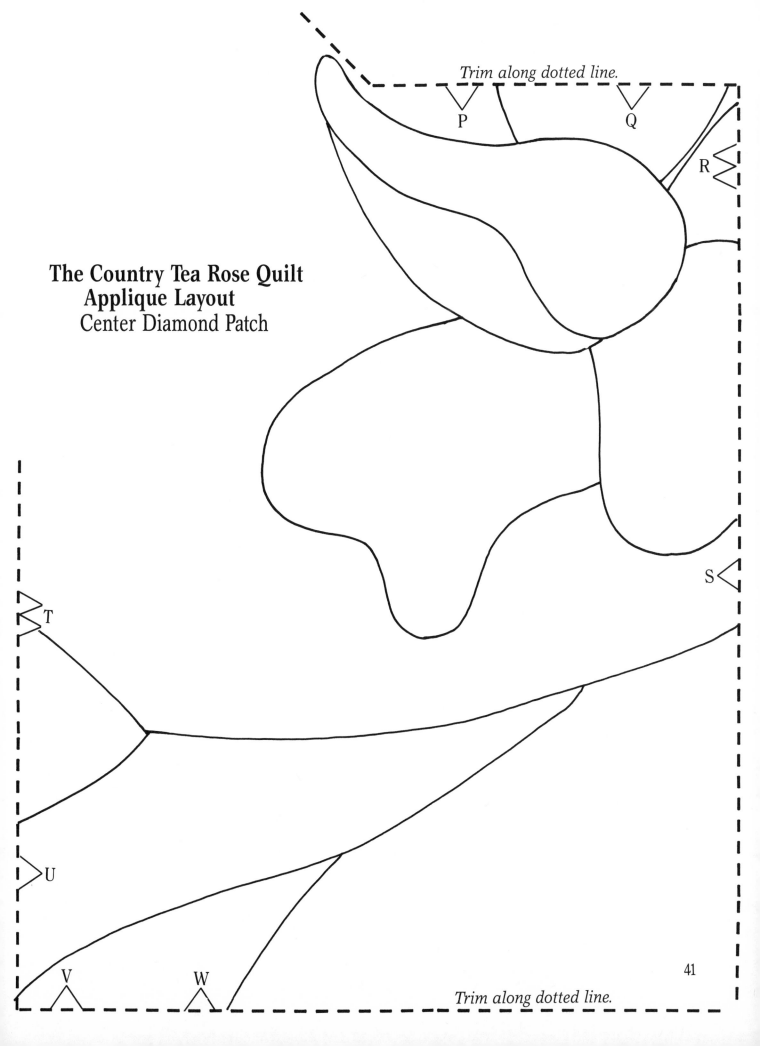

The Country Tea Rose Quilt
Applique Layout
Center Diamond Patch

Trim along dotted line.

P Q R S T U V W

41

Trim along dotted line.

The Country Tea Rose Quilt Applique Layout
Center Diamond Patch

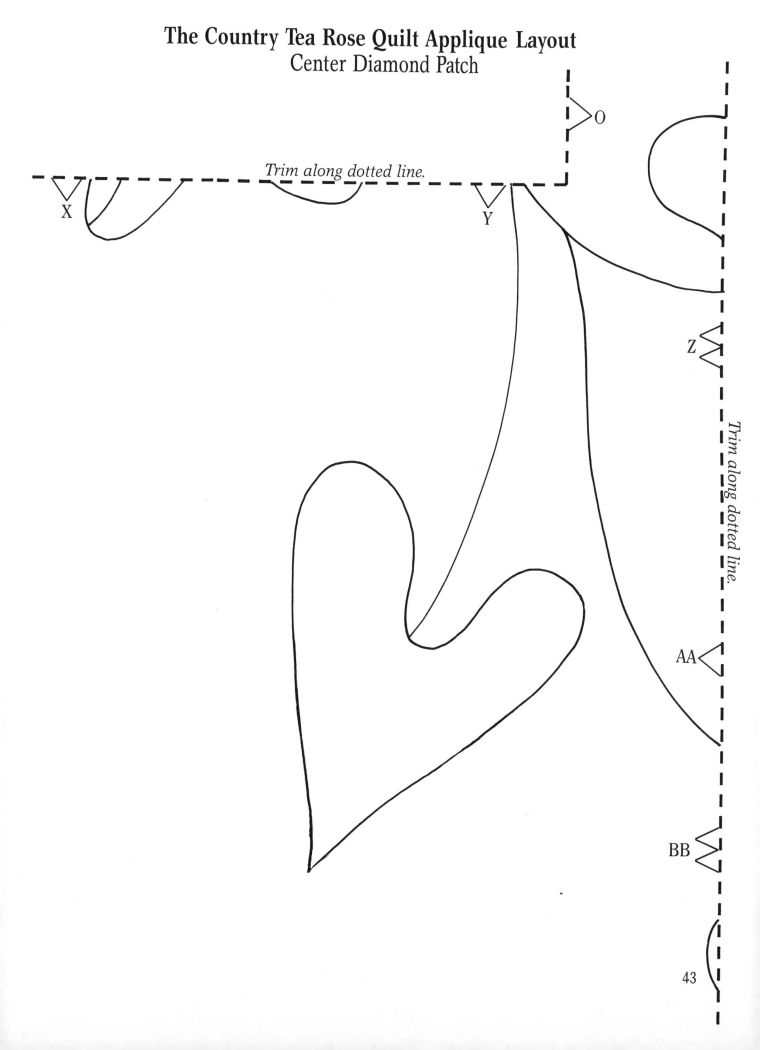

Trim along dotted line.

O

X

Y

Z

Trim along dotted line.

AA

BB

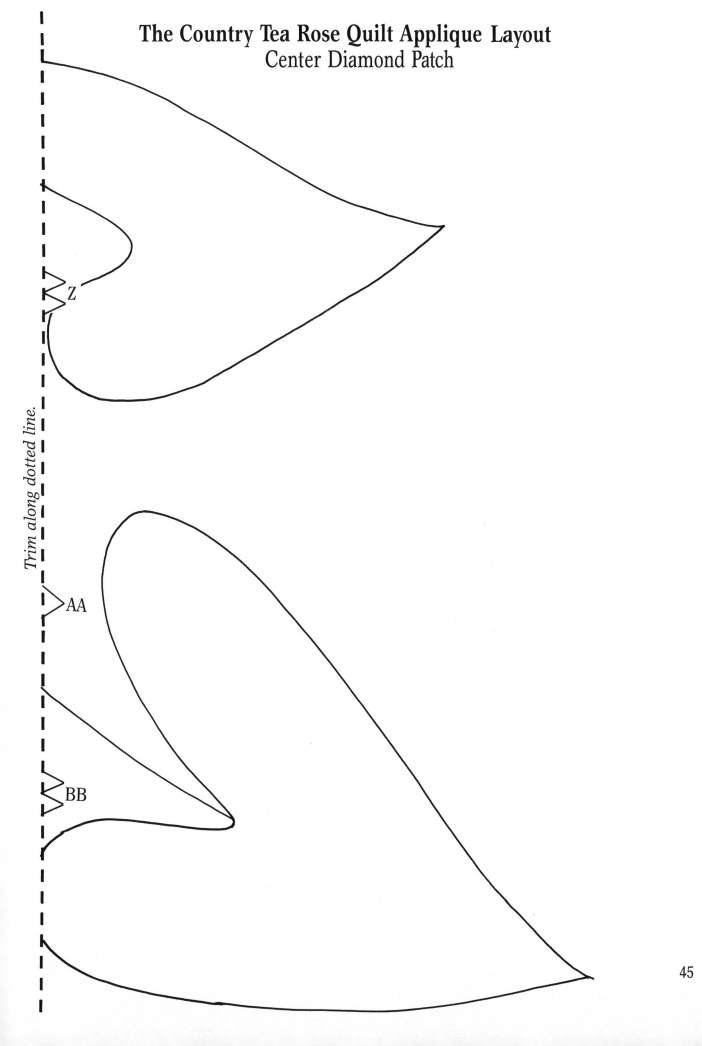

Trim along dotted line.

Z

AA

BB

The Country Tea Rose Quilt Applique Layout
Center Diamond Patch

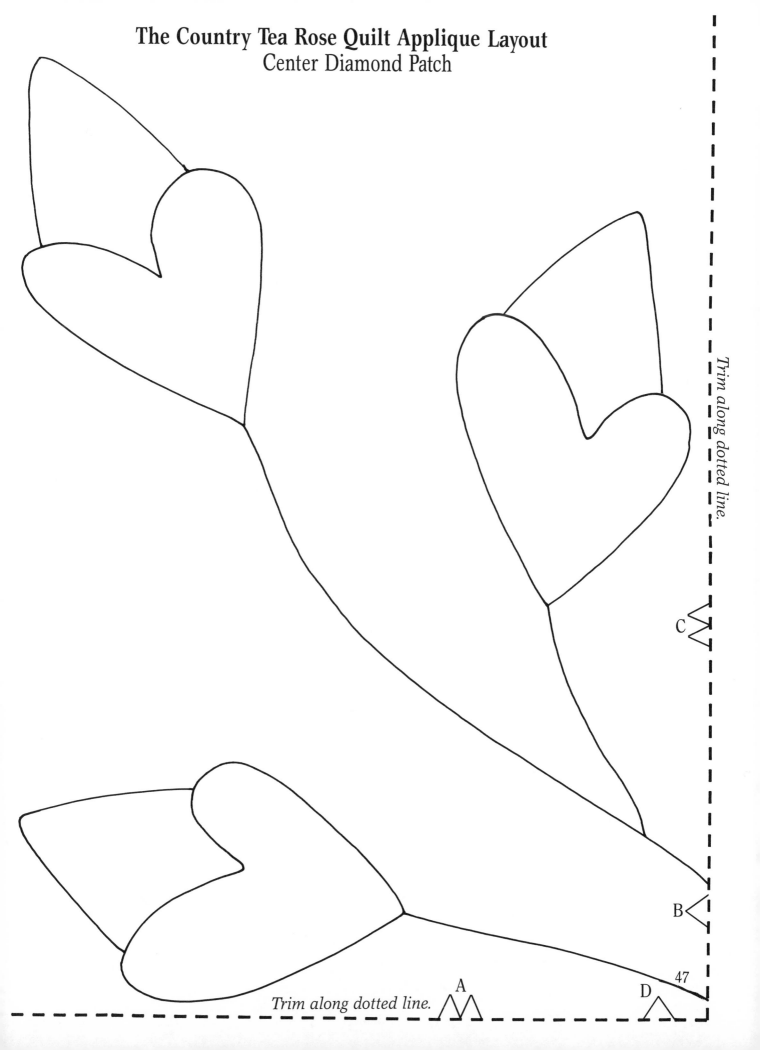

C

B

A

D

Trim along dotted line.

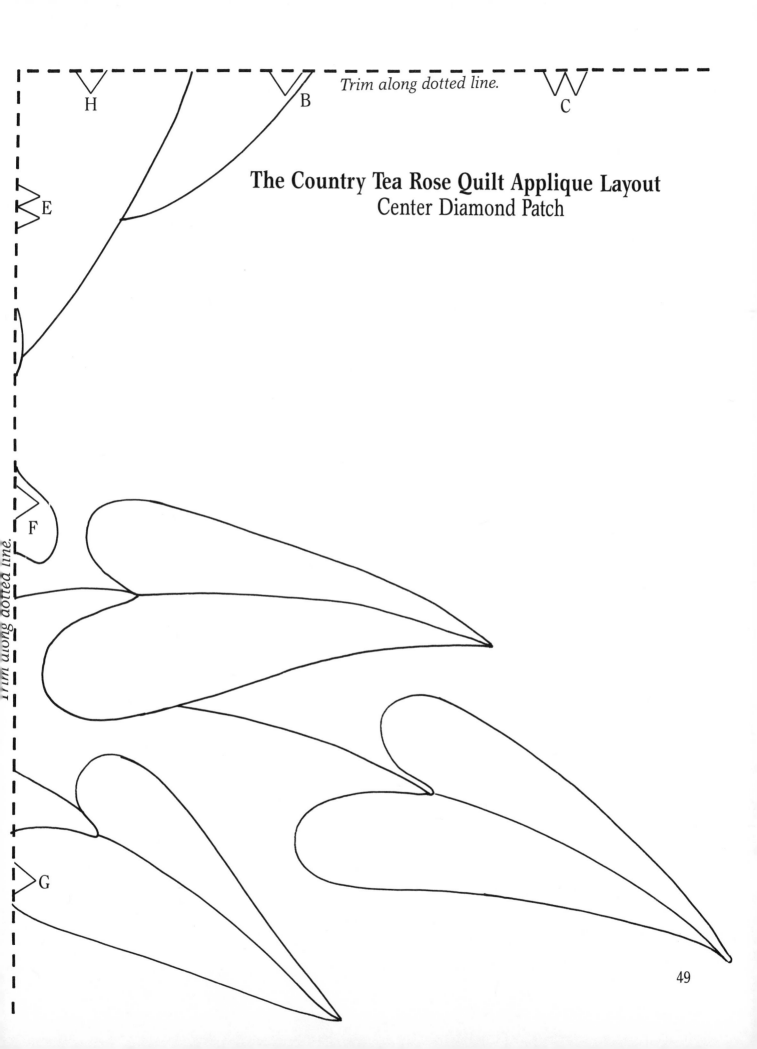

Trim along dotted line.

H

B

C

The Country Tea Rose Quilt Applique Layout
Center Diamond Patch

E

Trim along dotted line.

F

G

49

The Country Tea Rose Quilt Applique Layout

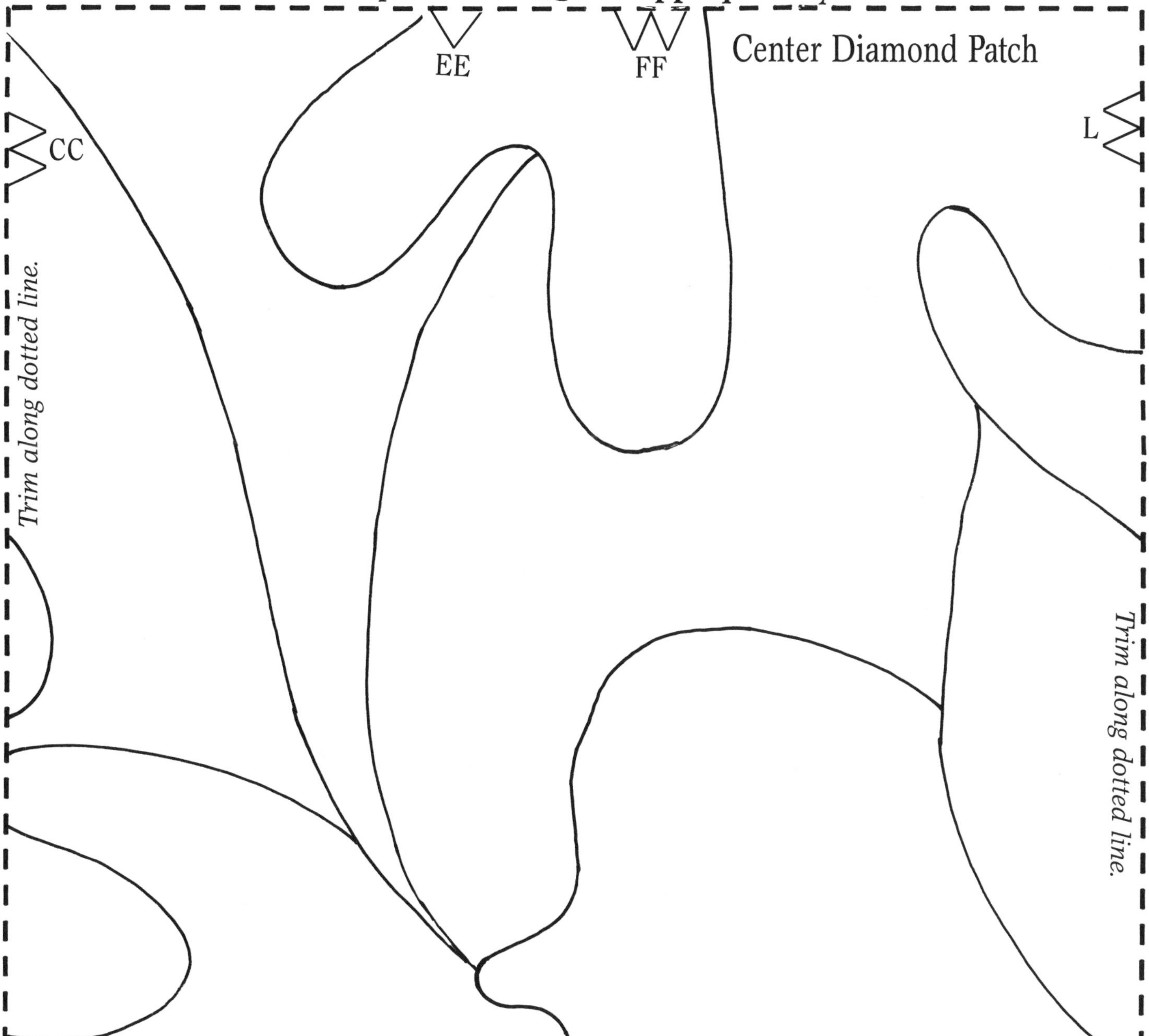

Center Diamond Patch

EE

FF

L

CC

Trim along dotted line.

Trim along dotted line.

DD

K

51

P

Q

N

M

The Country Tea Rose Quilt Applique Layout
Center Diamond Patch

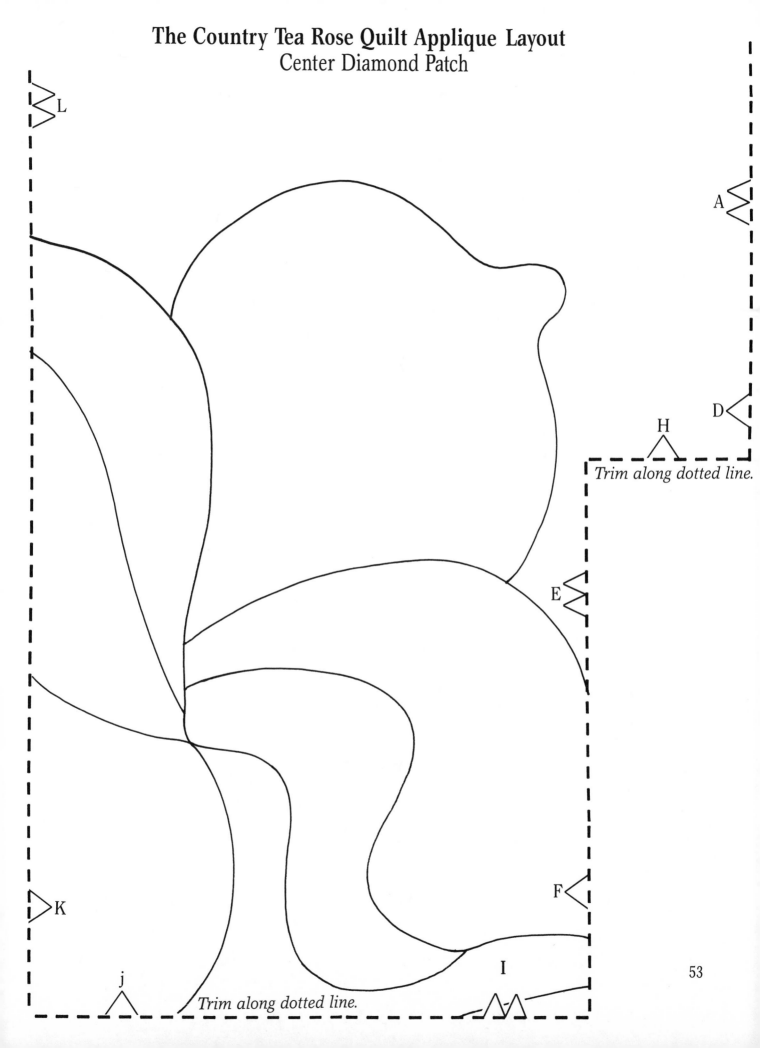

L

A

D

H

Trim along dotted line.

E

F

K

j

I

Trim along dotted line.

M

V

Trim along dotted line.

U

Trim along dotted line.

Trim along dotted line.

FF

EE

T

The Country Tea Rose Quilt Applique Layout

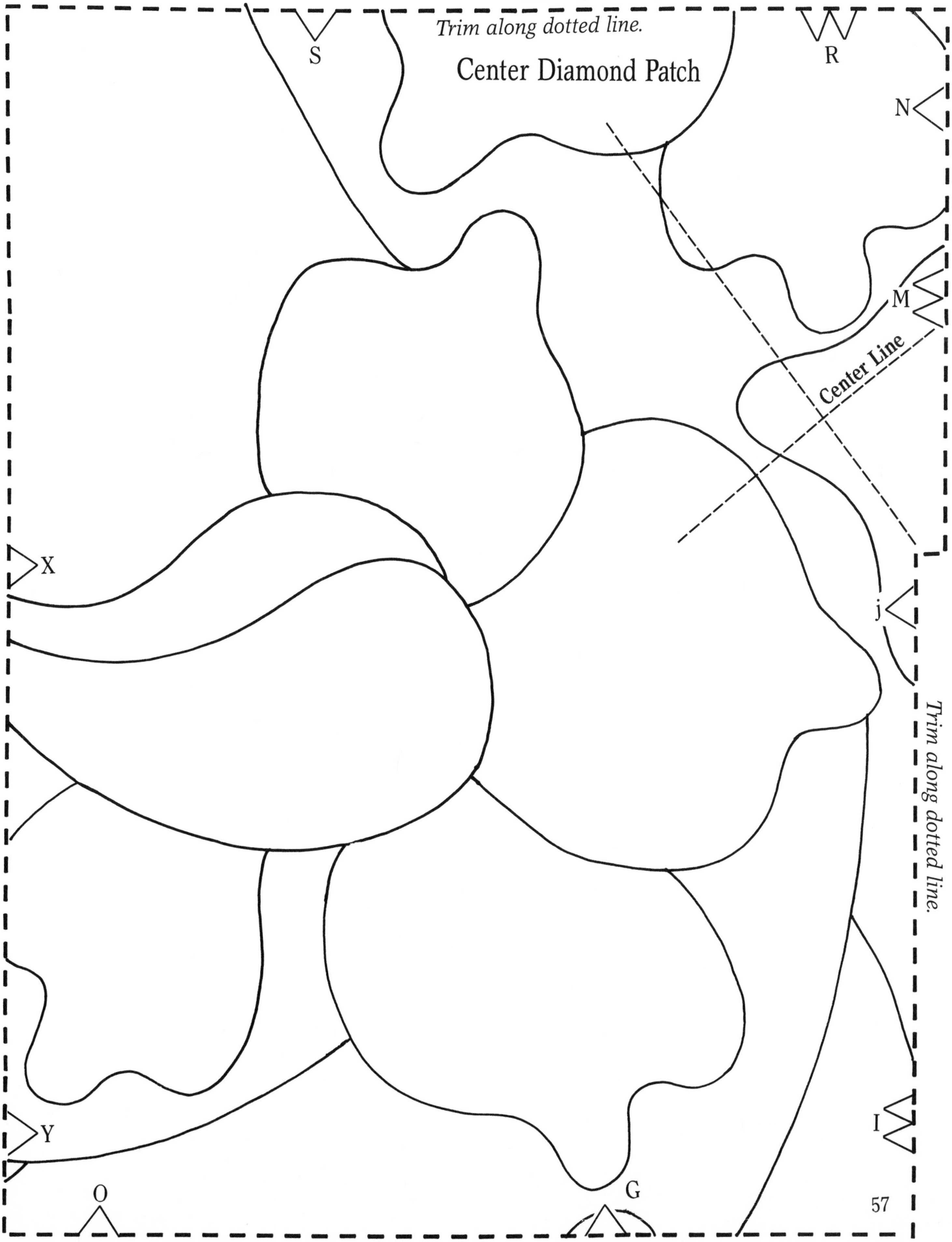

Trim along dotted line.

Center Diamond Patch

S

W

R

N

M

Center Line

X

j

Y

I

O

G

Trim along dotted line.

A

Trim along dotted line.

B

C

D

G

H

Trim along dotted line.

To create Corner Triangle/Pillow Throw layout, connect corresponding letters and notches along dotted lines and tape. Completed layout will look like this:

F

E

D

Trim along dotted line.

I

J

K

Trim along dotted line.

G

H

I

J

K

Trim along dotted line.

The Country Tea Rose Quilt Applique Layout
Corner Triangles/Pillow Throw

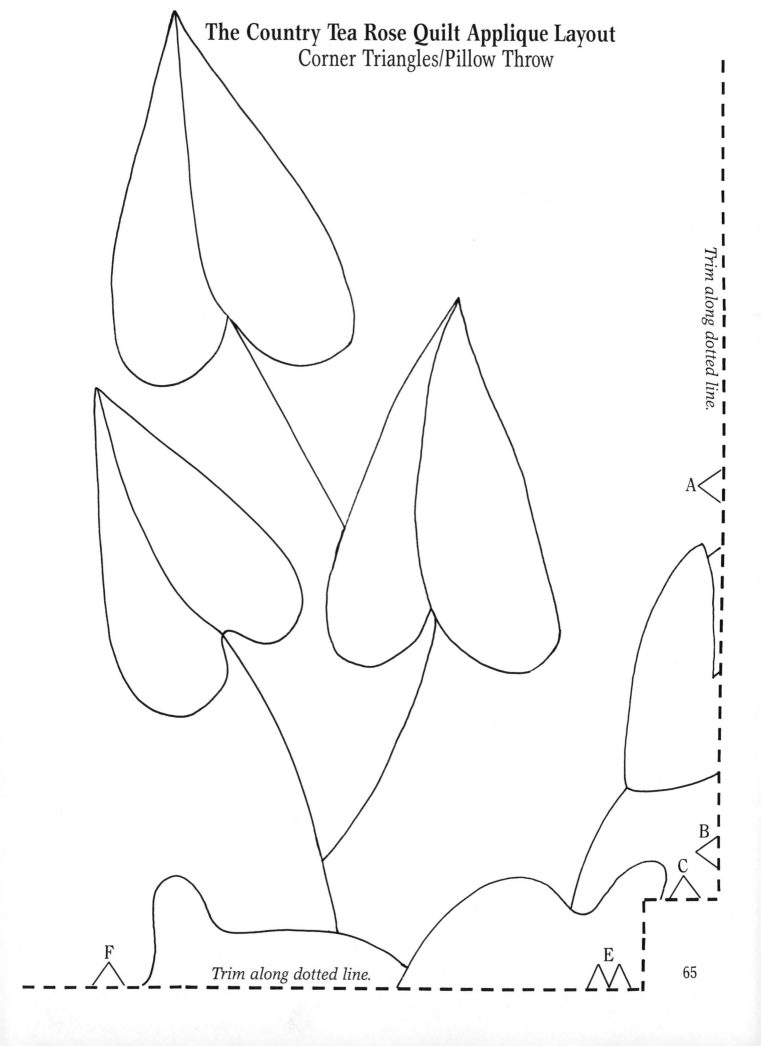

Trim along dotted line.

A

B

C

F

E

Trim along dotted line.

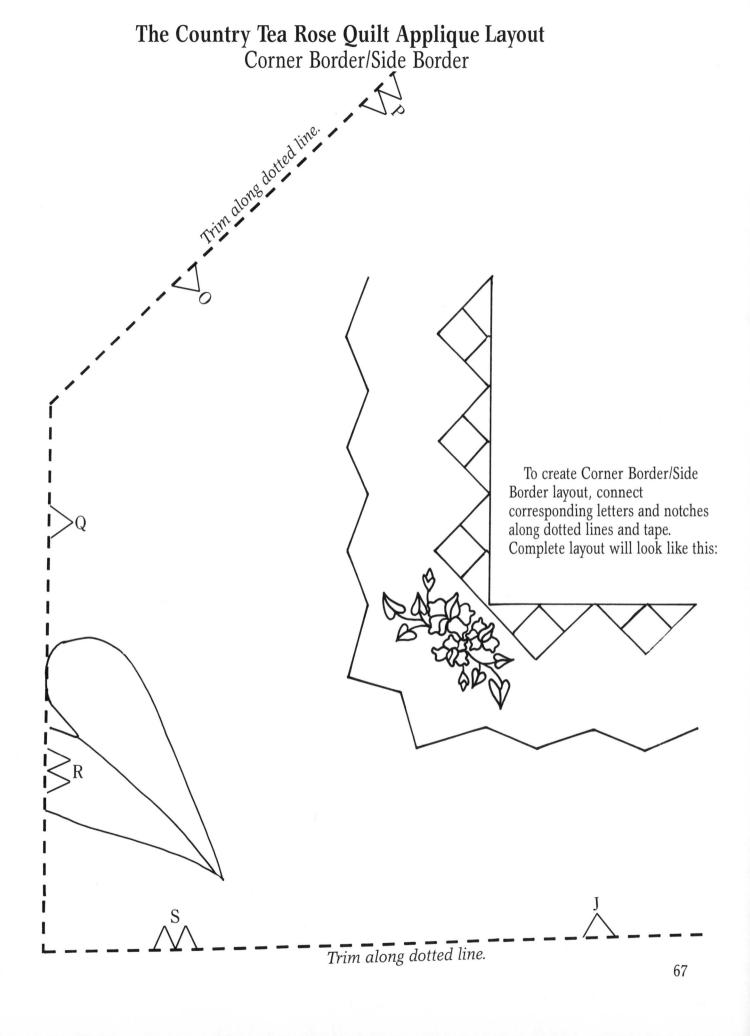

Trim along dotted line.

P

O

Q

To create Corner Border/Side Border layout, connect corresponding letters and notches along dotted lines and tape. Complete layout will look like this:

R

S

J

Trim along dotted line.

The Country Tea Rose Quilt Applique Layout
Corner Border/Side Border

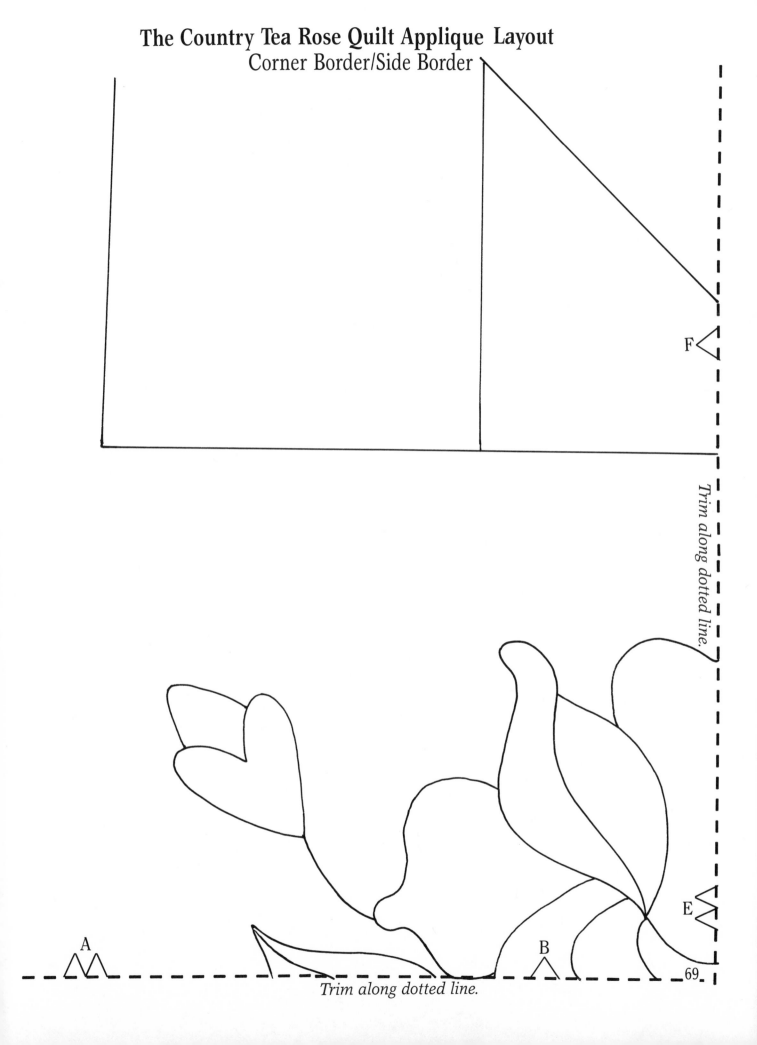

F

Trim along dotted line.

E

A

B

Trim along dotted line.

The Country Tea Rose Quilt Applique Layout

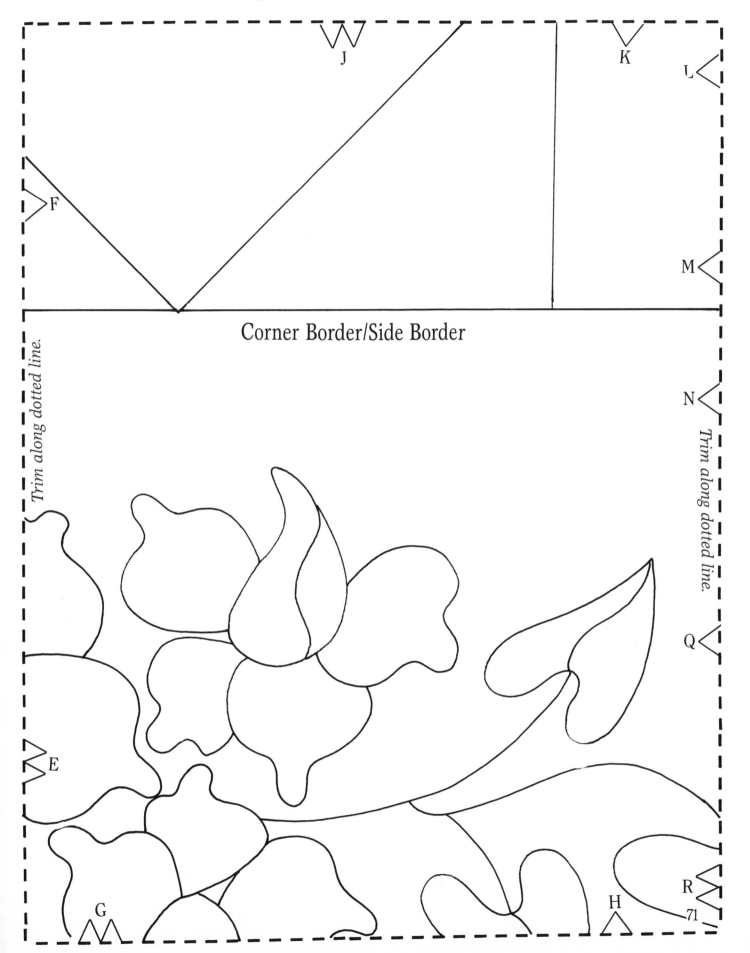

Corner Border/Side Border

Trim along dotted line.

Trim along dotted line.

W J

K

L

F

M

N

Q

E

G

H

R

71

The Country Tea Rose Quilt Applique Layout
Corner Border/Side Border

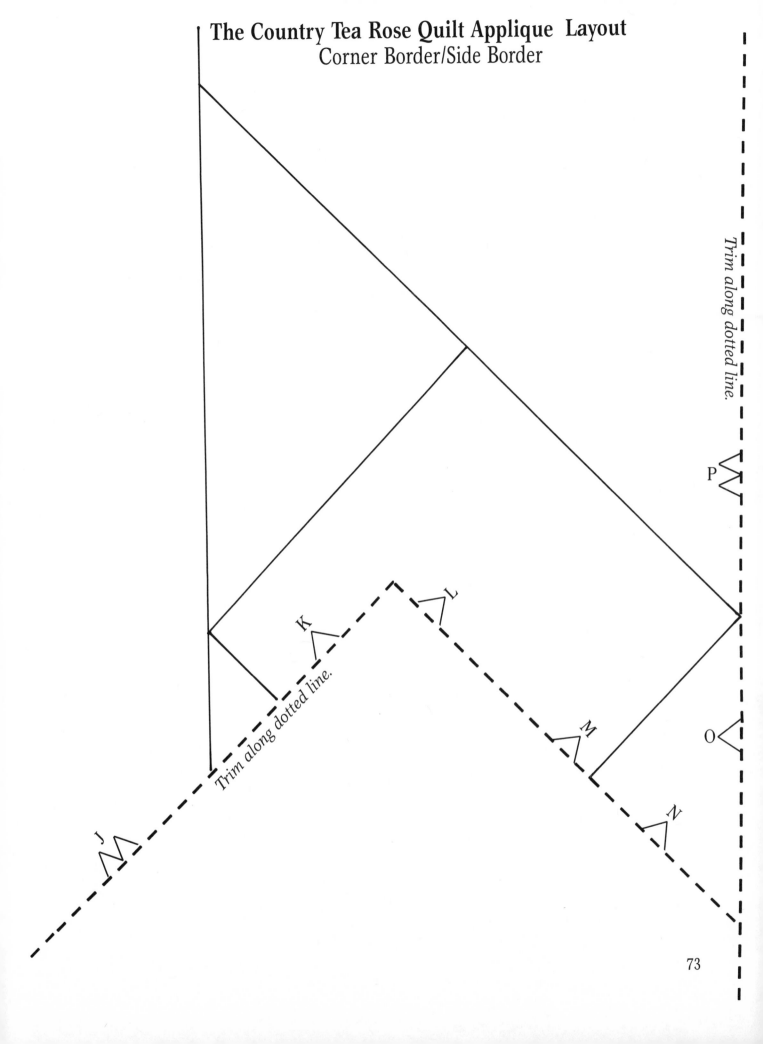

73

The Country Tea Rose Quilt Applique Layout
Corner Border/Side Border

Trim along dotted line.

G

C

I

H

U

D

Trim along dotted line.

V

The Country Tea Rose Quilt
Applique Layout
Corner Border/Side Border

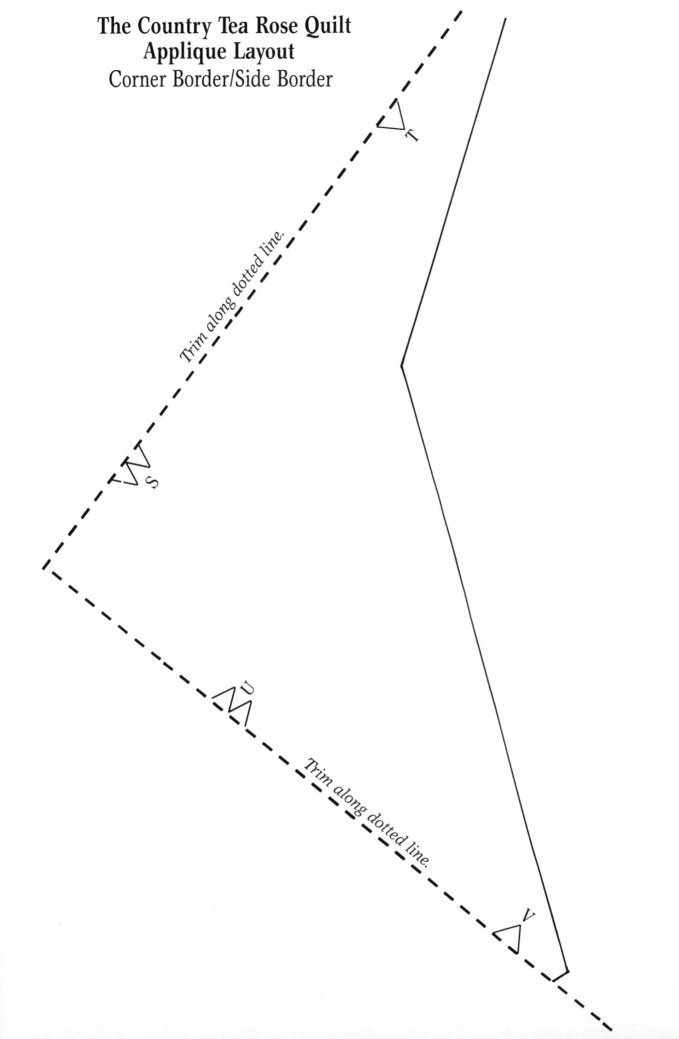

Trim along dotted line.

Trim along dotted line.

The Country Tea Rose Quilt Applique Layout
Corner Border/Side Border

Trim along dotted line.

A

B

C

I

Trim along dotted line.

D

79

Order Form

(all books are paperback)

Quantity

_____ copies of *The Country Bride Quilt* @ $12.95 each = $ _____

_____ copies of *The Country Bride Quilt Collection* @ $12.95 each = $ _____

_____ copies of *The Country Lily Quilt* @ $12.95 each = $ _____

_____ copies of *The Country Love Quilt* @ $12.95 each = $ _____

_____ copies of *The Country Paradise Quilt* @ $12.95 each = $ _____

_____ copies of *The Country Songbird Quilt* @ $12.95 each = $ _____

_____ copies of *Country Quilts for Children* @ $12.95 each = $ _____

_____ copies of *The Country Tea Rose Quilt* @ $12.95 each = $ _____

_____ copies of *Making Animal Quilts: Patterns and Projects*
         @ $12.95 each = $ _____

_____ copies of *Patterns for Making Amish Dolls and Doll Clothes*
         @ $12.95 each = $ _____

_____ copies of *Amish Quilt Patterns* @ $12.95 each = $ _____

_____ copies of *Small Amish Quilt Patterns* @ $12.95 each = $ _____

_____ copies of *Favorite Applique Patterns from The Old*
         Country Store, Volume 1 @ 15.95 = $ _____

_____ copies of *Favorite Applique Patterns from The Old*
         Country Store, Volume 2 @ 15.95 = $ _____

_____ copies of *Favorite Applique Patterns from The Old*
         Country Store, Volume 3 @ 15.95 = $ _____

_____ copies of *Favorite Applique Patterns from The Old*
         Country Store, Volume 4 @ 15.95 = $ _____

_____ copies of *Favorite Applique Patterns for the Holidays from*
         The Old Country Store, Volume 5 @ 15.95 = $ _____

_____ copies of *Favorite Applique Patterns from*
         The Old Country Store—Country Critters, Volume 6 @ 15.95 = $ _____

Subtotal _____

PA residents add 6% sales tax _____

Shipping and handling (Add 10%, $2.00 minimum) _____

TOTAL _____

METHOD OF PAYMENT

❏ Check or Money Order (payable to Good Books in U.S. funds)

❏ Please charge my:

     ❏ MasterCard   ❏ Visa

\# _____ exp. date _____

Signature _____

Name _____

Name _____

Address _____

City _____ State _____ Zip _____

Telephone (_____) _____

SHIP TO: (if different)

Name _____

Address _____

City _____ State _____ Zip _____

Telephone (_____) _____

Mail order to **Good Books**, P. O. Box 419, Intercourse, PA 17534;
Or call 1-800-762-7171 (in Canada, call collect 717/768-7171).
(Prices subject to change without notice.)

The People's Place Quilt Museum

About The Old Country Store

Cheryl A. Benner and Rachel T. Pellman are on the staff of The Old Country Store, located along Route 340 in Intercourse, Pennsylvania. The Store offers crafts from more than 300 artisans, most of whom are local Amish and Mennonites. There are quilts of traditional and contemporary designs, patchwork pillows and pillow kits, afghans, stuffed animals, dolls, tablecloths, and Christmas tree ornaments. Other handcrafted items include potholders, sunbonnets, and wooden toys.

For the do-it-yourself quilter, the Store offers quilt supplies, fabric at discount prices, and a large selection of quilt books and patterns.

Located on the second floor of the Store is The People's Place Quilt Museum. The Museum, which opened in 1988, features antique Amish quilts and crib quilts, as well as a small collection of dolls, doll quilts, socks, and other decorative arts.

About the Authors

Cheryl A. Benner and Rachel T. Pellman together developed the book, *The Country Tea Rose Quilt*. Benner created the patterns, then selected fabrics; together they supervised the making of the original quilts by Lancaster County Mennonite women. This is Benner's and Pellman's seventh collaboration on quilt designs with related books. Their earlier books are the popular *The Country Love Quilt, The Country Lily Quilt, The Country Songbird Quilt, The Country Bride Quilt Collection, The Country Paradise Quilt,* and *Country Quilts for Children,* and *Favorite Applique Patterns from the Old Country Store, Volumes 1 through 6.*

Benner, her husband Lamar, and two young sons live in Honeybrook, PA. She is a graduate of the Art Institute of Philadelphia (PA). Benner is art director for Good Enterprises, Intercourse, PA.

Pellman lives near Lancaster, PA and is manager of The Old Country Store, Intercourse. She is co-author of *The Country Bride Quilt*. She is also the author of *Tips for Quilters, Amish Quilt Patterns,* and *Small Amish Quilt Patterns;* co-author with Jan Steffy of *Patterns for Making Amish Dolls and Doll Clothes;* and co-author with her husband Kenneth of *A Treasury of Amish Quilts, The World of Amish Quilts, Amish Crib Quilts,* and *Amish Doll Quilts, Dolls and Other Playthings.*

The Pellmans are the parents of two sons.